Seeker of Silences

Also by Jussi Niittyviita

We Were Once Human
A Definition of Transcendence

A Year of Stillness
A Journey Into Inner Peace and Awakening

I Forgive You
An Unexpected Key to Awakening

7 Days of Presence
A Course in Inner Peace

The Sound of the Bells
A Story of the End of Suffering

An Inquiry Into Reality

More creations of peace and presence

available at www.jussiniittyviita.com

Seeker of Silences

Jussi Niittyviita

A seeker of silences am I,

and what treasure have I found in silences

that I may dispense with confidence?

- Kahlil Gibran

Contents

On Hoping for More 10

On Resisting Suffering 12

On Trusting in Not Knowing 14

On Imposing Unnecessary Judgments 16

On Feeling the Body as Myself 18

On Having Faith in Life 20

On Trusting Virtues 22

On Seeking Life from Tomorrow 24

On Experiencing the Present Moment 26

On Living for a Purpose 28

On Experiencing the Source of My Thoughts 30

On Facing Uncertainty 32

On Seeing Life as One Single Event 34

On Covering My Ears to Not Hear the Silence 36

On Paying Attention to My Experiences 38

On Enduring Frustration 40

On Listening to the Inner Echoes 42

On Loving Myself 44

On Approaching the Unknown 46

On Finding Wisdom in the Unhappiness 48

On Revealing Myself from Behind All the Symbols 50

On Moving to the Next Stop 52

On Being Aware of Impermanence 54

On Facing My Problems 56

On Seeing My Myriad Faces 58

On Listening to the Voice of My Mind 60

On Believing My Own Feelings 62

On Ceasing to Resist My Happiness 64

On Seeing My Connection to the World 66

On Understanding the Nature of My Experiences 68

On Noticing My Inner State of Lack 70

On Accepting My Fragments 72

On Following My Thoughts 74

On Touching the Present Moment 76

On Imagining the World as a Repetition 78

On Seeing the World in the Colors of a Rainbow 80

On Seeing Beyond My Life Situation 82

On Offering My Help for the World 84

On Experiencing Myself as Important 86

On Walking Along the Path of Consciousness 88

On Living Through Stories..90

On Falling in Love with My Feelings 92

On Giving Up the Need for Control..94

On Listening with the Ears of My Needs 96

On Choosing My Own Thoughts..98

On Seeing the True Nature of My Virtues 100

On Setting Aside My Knowledge 102

On Letting My Mind Grasp Thoughtlessness 104

On Trusting in My Search..106

On Being..108

On Hoping for More

The present moment is the seed of fulfillment.

Could I have hoped for more? When no answer is sought, the question answers itself. Everything is just the way it is because no other way exists. All moments in the waving ocean of time are meant to be just as they are, not as I would hope them to be. My own decisions have led me to this moment, whatever it holds within. I alone am the harbinger of my own experiences. Hope many times denies myself and the present moment—it is a false statement of lack.

Like all illusions, my hope also includes a promise of deeds. If I am wise enough to found my hope in the direct experience of *what is*, and what I am, my deeds will sow seeds of fulfillment. Time flows and the conditions will change. Eventually, my experience of *what is* approaches my hope. It happens carefully at first, but over time, my hope shakes hands with my experience like old friends. Thus, I regain my once forgotten friendship with myself.

Continuous acceptance of the present moment caresses the seed of fulfillment until it bursts into a flower. My experience of the present moment is the purpose of existence. If a flower unfolds and reveals its beauty before my eyes, then my experience of beauty is the purpose of the flower. If the flower withers, it becomes an image of death and decay. In turn, my experience of death and decay is the purpose of the flower.

When I understand the flower, I can realize the freedom in my life. It is not freedom as a spiritual or physical concept, but something much deeper. Despite the conditions, I am free to experience everything I do. I am free to experience my own world. That freedom whispers of my hope to the ears of the world, and the world echoes my whispers back in its own unique way.

The world answers my hope without hesitation or judgment, with acceptance and love. But it does so only if I treat myself with unwavering acceptance and love. I find the answer to the question "Could I have hoped for more?" in the peace and silence within. There is nothing left to hope for. I have everything I will ever need *'here and now'*.

On Resisting Suffering

If I resist my suffering, I empower it to destroy me.

I am prone to feeling psychological pain and suffering. It might appear as an inconspicuous grain of irritation, or more prominent anxiety. Whenever suffering stares into my soul with its burning eyes, I feel it at full capacity; it is not relative, but always pure, pristine, sincere, and it devours all the space within.

I cannot escape my suffering through thinking: "It is not as bad as it seems. I have experienced worse than this. Millions of people in the world are in a worse situation than I am. I know someone who has been through the same." Avoiding, denying, and resisting the feeling of suffering using the tools of thinking only empowers the feeling.

I can see through my suffering only when facing it directly. Facing my suffering does not mean acknowledging its external causes, but gazing into the relentless eyes of the feeling of suffering. As I approach the feeling itself, its eyes burn my own eyes like a thousand suns. They scorch my spirit to ashes. They imprison me in dark and lifeless dungeons bearing the names of fear, hate, anxiety, grief, regret, and worry.

However, beyond all that, after walking through all the agony, I merge to my feeling. I become aware of something that has been in the background all the time—compassion. It is not the limited compassion created by my mind, but something happening deeper within me. That compassion is without an object, and therefore all objects are embraced by it, including my suffering.

Because I hold the ability to feel suffering within me, I can also feel it in another. The suffering in the purest form is the same in all living beings as it is in me. Therefore, I feel compassion for all living beings. When I try to resist or avoid my suffering, I am escaping the world around me, and escaping from the world means denying myself.

I can release myself from the prison of my suffering only by stepping closer to the feeling of it. In the silence of the mind, I can do so with unlimited compassion.

On Trusting in Not Knowing

My knowledge is a self-made prison.

I often believe I hold the truth of a multitude of things. But do I really know anything about them? I spend a big part of my life in an inner world driven by knowledge. I mistake to believe knowledge is the reality, and during that same breath, I unconsciously produce a false image of myself. One of permanence, rooted in limited knowledge.

I am gazing at the snowfall in front of me. My mind has formed an image of it, but do I really know what a snowfall looks like? In the silent night sky, I can see clusters of bright stars arising from the embrace of the black space. But have I ever actually seen the light of the stars? I feel like a mind attached to a body, a totality I call my personality, but have I ever truly felt my body or my mind? In the moments of inner peace and silence, a question arises: "What is the 'I' that can feel myself?"

My thoughts represent the world in their own straightforward way. They create symbolic images of what the world looks like. Arising with the mental images of the world, a symbol of myself arises—the 'I' who is looking at the world through the kaleidoscope of my knowledge. If my knowledge of the world defines who I am, then at the same fleeting moment, what I don't know also defines who

I am. Am I therefore everything? My knowledge might create an identity, but it is rarely myself.

The nature of all knowledge is ephemeral. I can only observe its rising and falling, like leaves of the tree appear in spring and wither away in autumn. When the leaves have withered, all that is left is not knowing.

I feel insignificantly small when I think about the volume of what I do not know. However, in that state of insignificance, I can open the mental fist I was unconsciously clenching. Letting go of my knowledge makes space for creation. In the stillness of the mind, I can lean backward, relax, and see life before my eyes as a play, which seamlessly integrates to a much vaster play of existence.

My role is crucial in that play, regardless of my feelings of insignificance. I am unique simply because I exist. Any knowledge added to simply existing blurs the vision of myself and creates false significance. Without my small and insignificant role, the whole play would crumble down in its own impossibility.

Relying on the warm and free embrace of not knowing is challenging because too often I need to invoke my knowledge. But the situation is not dire; only by invoking my knowledge can I experience what the boundless embrace of not knowing feels like.

On Imposing Unnecessary Judgments

Whatever I judge in another is my own ignorance.

When I know exactly who I am, without any doubt of myself, I tend to judge the world around me. I impose my judgments on events, conditions, and especially other people. I continuously need to assess the outside world in relation to myself, and as a result, the world feels like a threat to my own survival. That vague and elusive feeling of threat defines much of my identity, and all identities are prone to impose unnecessary judgments.

No light or heavy judgments arise in the endless vortices of my soul. There are only judgments that exist, and in our existence, they are all alike. None of my thoughts are truly neutral or nonjudgmental, even though I would like to believe so.

My thought that addresses the beauty of the shimmering sunset, which colors the whole skyline with hues of bright orange, is fundamentally no different than my thought that addresses the cruelty of the most hideous and murderous human being in existence. Whenever a thought arises in my consciousness, the mechanical process of the mind judges the thought beneficial or harmful to myself. Everything that feels beneficial or harmful is only an expression of my accumulated knowledge, a mirage in the realm of time.

When judging the world around me, I am actually judging myself. Many times I believe I know the truth, but the other side of the truth holds everything I do not know. If I were someone else, lived in a different time or place, or my life situation was different, I would be part of my current ignorance. Deep within, in the silence of my soul, I am my knowledge and my ignorance.

The best I can do for myself is to continuously find a way to see the two sides of myself: the seemingly real 'I', which is small, limited, fragile, and based on my knowledge, and the 'self' that is everything else. Together they form the being who I am. Only when the mind falls silent, I can truly accept my ignorance, which is a significant part of me.

On Feeling the Body as Myself

Dysfunction of thinking produces a false identity.

I cannot point to any exact part of the body that I could exclusively label as myself. My identity is created somewhere else than in the body, and the body is only an object of it. In the embrace of an identity, all objects are rendered to concepts of what they actually are.

Most parts of the body are beyond the reaches of my thoughts. I usually pay attention to the body only when it is strained, broken, or somehow in a state of a malfunction. However, those conditions cover just an insignificant part of it all. The significant part of it—that which keeps the body up and running—has a transient and unknown nature.

I cannot directly sense the essential parts of the body. I can only feel some derivative sensations of them. I can feel the heart beating in my chest, but not the heart itself. I can feel the warm tingling in my toes and fingertips, but not the flow of the blood within them. I can see the world around me, but my eyes are invisible to me. I can hear the world, but my ears are silent. However, when the body is in malfunction, I identify with the faulty functionality quite easily—I feel any malfunction as a part of myself, that must be fixed.

The body and mind are intrinsically connected. No definite dividing lines seem to exist where the body is not the mind, or the mind is not the body. Are my thoughts, therefore, similar malfunctions of the mind, just as malfunctions appear in the body? Is my essential nature found when there is no dysfunction of thinking present? Am I the best version of myself when I do not know to be myself? When I do not sense my identity, there is no irritation, hatred, jealousy, fear, or the clinging kind of love the mind is prone to fall into.

To fulfill my part in the totality of the mind and body, I must merge with it. I must jump into the stream this totality creates, leaving my sense of identity behind. In the silence of the mind, I can let things be just as they are without my personal investment in the equation.

On Having Faith in Life

I can see my faithful self in the absence of truths.

If I was looking at life from the perspective of a bird, everything would seem fundamentally different. I would value entirely different things. My feelings and thoughts would be profoundly different if they even existed like they do now.

I would live for food, survival, reproduction, the rustle of the wind under my wings, and the embrace of the open sky around my weightless body. I could feel the wind on my face and see the ground far below me, covered with green forests, clear hills, and deep waters. I could feel the sweet ecstasy of being, which holds no equivalent in power on the level of thinking.

The experience I call 'my life' is the sum of all the learned views and selected memories that create the reality around me. I'm mistaken to believing such reality as the truth. I easily forget that an infinite amount of different truths exist in the world. There are countless birds beside me soaring through the open sky. However, sometimes I forget every single truth the world bestows upon me. In the haven of those silent moments, I am freedom.

Without freedom, I am destined to perceive everything through a thick lens of my thoughts and mental positions. They dictate how I experience a world that

already wanes into the past when I try to make sense of it.
My past is a memory I look through that same lens. As I
think about my life, even the future, I actually think about
my past. As I stop thinking, I experience reality.

The world's true nature unfolds when I dare to
look deep into the world's soul. It is a mirror in which I can
see myself. I am because existence gives birth to something
I can observe. In such moments of simple existence and
inner silence, the faith in the world *is*.

On Trusting Virtues

All virtues have their counterforces.

Even the smallest good deed carries within it an unknown seed of destruction. It remains hidden because of my limited thinking. I love to commit virtues that produce satisfaction for myself, my loved ones, my acquaintances, and sometimes also for people I am not involved with. Additionally, many times, I tend to choose virtues that make me feel less guilty.

Behind the scenes, beyond the limitations of my knowledge, every virtuous act is affected by forces I cannot entirely understand. My virtuous deeds are often based on a hidden fear. A fear that smolders somewhere deep within the mind. When I act driven by that fear, I might succeed in producing good results temporarily, but the fear will inevitably manifest in some another way. The primordial forces of fear and love always find their way to form their physical equivalents in the world.

I inherently seek instant results for my deeds. As I commit virtuous acts, I expect to see the evil overthrown by my grandeur. However, my expectations, which are constructed from the experiences of my past, blind me from seeing a greater totality. Blinded, I cannot see how many of my seemingly virtuous deeds actually represent nothing more than my fears.

I sincerely believe I am a good person. When I grab a weapon and go to war, demons will run with full certainty. But they never run without a price. It is a price that I have committed to pay with my unconscious virtues. Every justified war has its victims. The most sacred and pristine virtue is the one I commit without a virtuous purpose.

On Seeking Life from Tomorrow

Sometimes I live in a state of mind I mistake for a future.

Time is a ball of yarn that seems to have unfolded on my path. The unfolded yarn holds within the memories of yesterdays and the expectations of tomorrows. However, any perspective feels like the one and only moment, the center of the path. In that moment, I exist '*here and now*'.

My experiences indicate strongly that all my past deeds affect my future. Through such experiences, I constantly weave together a form of myself. This form depends on how all the loops of the yarn are woven into it. Despite the causal nature of the form, all the loops are always included in the moment called '*now*'. My life happens in time, yet it is timeless. My mind goes into gridlock when trying to think about that intrinsically conflicting totality. When I do not try to think about it, I can feel the peace and silence it carries within.

My life can never happen in tomorrow. It never has and it never will. The meaning of my existence is fulfilled only in the infinite continuum of the present moment. The finished form that is woven of the unfolded ball of yarn is still essentially the same original ball in which there is no distinction between the concepts of before and after. The loops of time that my hands weave to produce diverse forms are a by-product of the unceasing mechanical process of my mind. The process has its place in the world because it exists similarly as I do, but the time it creates is merely an illusion.

Tomorrow is real only in the present moment. Why should I use any more time to think about it than the fulfillment of the present moment needs me to?

On Experiencing the Present Moment

Clinging to the illusion of time creates a profound misunderstanding.

All my memories and expectations occur inside the moment called '*now*'. I give birth to that moment and everything in it by simply existing. The reality I experience could never be without me. If I create my reality while dependent on the image of the past, I destroy what I call the free will. Free will can never exist as a result of memories because living through memories is the eternal repetition of the past. There is no freedom in the past.

The illusion of time is created in my mind. Whenever I contemplate the present moment, that moment has already vanished, like how the form of a snowflake instantly vanishes on my warm palm. All that remains is a vivid memory of the snowflake, an echo which slowly fades into nothingness.

My life is a continuous struggle to grasp the present moment, or worse, to avoid it by plunging into the chaotic vortices of the stream of thinking. If I try to grasp the present moment, it will flee from me always and forever, and I lose the actual nature of it. If I want to avoid the present moment and allow excessive thinking, I forget about its existence entirely. However, all the losing and forgetting are rendered meaningless at the very instant I stop trying.

The reality is an experience, not a happening. It has no beginning or end. All seemingly separate time-bound happenings are actually one indefinitely vast event, washing over existence like a giant wave at the same time and place everywhere. As I cease to grasp the concept of time with force, I find the actual nature of the present moment. The nature of the present moment is always pristine and sacred, independent of memories and expectations. It is independent of my identity and the seemingly free decisions I make through my identity.

Like the flower rises up from the seed without any chains of the experience of time, I also grow as a flower of the existence. Whether I accept it or not is not my choice, because I am that. Whether I will do it consciously is my choice. Conscious of it all, I can see that all flowers open their petals to the sun and eventually wither away. Over time, and on time.

On Living for a Purpose

When I breathe, I meet my ultimate purpose.

The world does not include anything in vain or without meaning. A flower reaching for the blue sky in the silent meadow does not strive to be anything else than a flower. It lives for its own beauty because it is beautiful in itself. A river winding through the land does not feel any more worthwhile or useless because it is only a river. It does not need to be anything else. Despite the harmonious nature around me, I am cursed with the idea of becoming.

The 'I' inside me compares the world as beneficial or harmful to me. It insists on striving for a benefit and avoiding harm. When external things affect me, the 'I' leaves me no other option than to define those external things in relation to myself. In the embrace of that relative experience, my life gains a temporary purpose. It is a kind of purpose whose gravity might grow irresistible over the years, be it beneficial or harmful.

My temporary purpose has many faces. It can lead me to thinking good thoughts, or it can manifest my most dreadful nightmares. Many times, I can see my temporary purpose looking at me in the mirror with eyes that are not my own. Stranger's eyes. However, the causes and effects of my temporary purpose cover only a grain of the purpose I hold within.

Whenever a temporary purpose arises through relative experiences, at the same time my inner purpose arises. A purpose which is infinitely the same. A purpose that is loving, open, and compassionate. A purpose of existing. If I am not aware of it, I become a prisoner of the world. As I become aware of my inner purpose, my breath flows free. I take the temporary purpose consciously in my embrace, become one with it, and eventually, I let it go into the fading waves of the past.

Just like the flower has a purpose of being a flower, and the river has a purpose of being a river, also my purpose is to be a full-fledged human being in the everlasting moment of presence. The very foundation for being a human is to breathe. As I breathe, I fulfill my deepest purpose in this moment.

On Experiencing the Source of My Thoughts

My thoughts create illusory forms of separation.

My thoughts constantly change their form. They create a strange and yet realistic sense of identity. Just like the transparent raindrops fall on the surface of the lake in the summer and fragile snowflakes land on the thick cover of ice in the winter, so too do my thoughts gain different forms depending on the conditions. The mind composes different meanings out of those forms. My experience as an identity is the sum of all those meanings.

Deep under the surface, in the embrace of the icy blanket of winter, water is always water. Deep within me, my thoughts are born of the same source, utterly independent of the forms and meanings I give to them. The building material of my thoughts is always the same, even though they gain forms of complex expressions of love and fear when examined afterward.

One thought is a snowflake—how can I ever see inside the heart of it when my vision is obscured by the snowfall? How can I know the soothing darkness of the lake when I am blinded by the white snow-covered ice? In the suffocating embrace of my thinking, I look at the world through the meanings created by the sophisticated mechanisms of the mind. I have created my identity as a symbol of the world in relation to me. It is a creation of limited thoughts and feelings called the 'I'.

However, my life is not always filled with the noise of thinking. During such moments, the snow and ice are altogether water. My thoughts still rise and fall, but I do not look at the world through their distorting lens. I do not create a separation between the water, snow, and ice, but I let them be and exist just as they are. Through this I become aware that when I do not cling to their meanings, they are born of the same source.

I become my thoughts when they rain thousandfold from the vast sky above me. But *I am* when the sky is bright and unclouded.

On Facing Uncertainty

A shadow of doubt looms over everything but the

present moment.

I have cursed myself to live in a constant state of uncertainty. Nothing in the realms of time can bestow upon me the certainty I deeply long for. Reaching for certainty is a paradox. Nothing I achieve will last, and the more I reach and grasp, the further I drift from what I am trying to grasp. Time will take care of that.

Everything time-bound is extremely uncertain. I look at the past through the reflections of my mental positions. The image of the past in my mind is a faded canvas full of holes which contains more empty space than canvas itself. If I cannot be certain of my own past experiences, then what can I be really certain of?

The present moment—which is entirely free of any ideas of becoming—is the only certainty in this world. It is all that is happening *now*. Settling in the present moment does not mean the stopping of time, or ignorance, or absent-mindedness, but a total and relentless acceptance of this forever flowing moment. It grants me wisdom, born in the heart of all possible uncertainty.

When I can trust that the eternal certainty of existence lasts now and forever, I can accept the eternal uncertainty of time. In the embrace of that acceptance, I will not only endure the suffering created by the time-bound uncertainty, but I will expel it into nonexistence. The erasing of suffering is the key to trust and gratitude, which opens the doorless door to limitless compassion. And compassion for myself is my essential nature.

On Seeing Life as One Single Event

As I watch and listen attentively, the present moment

divides no past or future.

My memories create an undefined feeling of a direction, pointing from my past towards my future. The direction exists, however, only in the present moment. The moment called '*now*' includes nothing separate from other things. No event is separate from another event. The '*now*' forms by itself like a group of geese form a wedge in their flight across the bright blue sky—without thinking and planning; driven by a pure purpose of being. The present moment forms in the same way, over, and over, and over again, without beginning or ending.

The events I ceaselessly experience '*now*' form a bridge between my memories and expectations. The bridge is masoned from thoughts, beliefs, mental positions, and all the feelings they produce. Standing on that bridge, I divide my life into the past and future. I create my direction. All events that feel separate from each other are the separation in my mind.

Occasionally, I can feel the events following some greater pattern than just themselves. In that pattern, they are no longer separate, but intrinsically and seamlessly woven together. The chain of events is an infinite continuum of interconnections. They merge into one another, creating a rhythm whose immense complexity cannot be contemplated with the limited tools of my mind. Carried by this rhythm, my life feels like a timeline squeezed into an infinitesimal point, where all events occur at the same time and in the same place. That point is insignificantly small in the cosmic scale. However, I do not feel small or insignificant because all significance draws its existence from insignificance.

The moment called '*now*' is one immeasurably great event. It exists only because I am here to witness its existence. My experience of the present moment creates a purpose for it, and at the same time, it creates a purpose for me. Neither one of us can exist without the other. I am tied to a love story that never gains the strength to become revealed if I write it based on my past or future. The love, however, echoes in the background with every breath I take, no matter what actions I commit or what beliefs I hold within.

Like the distant cry of a bird over the still lake creates meaning for the silence, I also create this moment out of stillness and silence.

On Covering My Ears to Not Hear the Silence

Sometimes I fear the silence and stillness, but the fear is not who I am.

Death is quiet at the moment of its arrival. In death, I disappear into the silence that echoes in the background of the play of existence. During the moments when my thoughts stop, I die. My mind is afraid of death, and it does everything it can to prevent me from hearing the silence. It fights the silence with all the power it has. However, in silence, all my thoughts fade away like the morning mist over the field disappears with the rays of the rising sun.

My mind occasionally tortures me with suffering and anxiety. They tend to press my posture down and lower my eyes to the ground. My mind whispers enchanting and fearful words to me that I many times mistake with having a sense of myself. The curse of the human mind is that thoughts occur inevitably, whether they cause pleasures or sufferings. However, in their purest form, no occurrence in the world is any better than it is worse. I create the experience of good and bad myself.

When I try to force my thoughts to disappear, they strengthen. When I try to pull back from them, they pull back with me towards the silence, never reaching it. My most humble effort to settle in a thoughtless state of mind inevitably results in a mental position where my effort becomes my thought. This effort lingers hidden somewhere in the back of the skull. It is a crest so large in the ocean of thoughts that I do not always notice its presence.

Paradoxically, if I do not try to stop the stream of thought, the thoughts cease by themselves through simple awareness. It happens suddenly, without any warning, and in situations where I least expect it to happen. In those moments the 'I' disappears, and the most essential part of silence emphasizes everything that is not silence. I realize that the world and its infinite emptiness arise mutually into existence.

The effort in covering my ears to not hear the silence is born out of the fear of death in the endless waves of my thoughts. What if 'I' disappear? What if 'I' cannot find my way back? However, there is no way back. I am already home.

On Paying Attention to My Experiences

My identity exists before or after the world around me.

I have a tendency to prejudge things, events, and especially other people. My mind creates experiences even before I arrive in a given situation. All experiences I have in advance—prejudices before a particular situation—are but echoes from the past. They are beliefs that inhibit the arising of my pure and natural experiences. The belief system that I usually call *'my life'* obscures the real experience of my life.

I constantly look at the wake of my boat, as it slowly fades and merges into the stillness of the ocean. Similarly, all my prejudices are the faded past within, and that past is unknown to me. In the state of ignorance, I blindly commit actions that are dictated by the unknown past. Those unconscious actions imprison me in a dungeon, whose walls are painted with illusory images of time. As a prisoner of time, I am also the prisoner of the world. Prisoners of the world have no free will, but only a delusion of free will. Many times I mistakenly believe the free will as my own, but in reality, it is someone else's will whispered from the unknown past. Where is my freedom in fulfilling the dreams of my predecessors, or avoiding their fears?

What I have seen in the wake of my strange boat creates what I will see under the bow of the boat. The bow that is dividing the strange waters in front of me. I usually become aware of my experiences only afterward, when my mind has piled up all the weight of the past on my pure experience. As I open my eyes and watch the world as it kneels before me, I can understand that the future I many times expect with bright and awaiting eyes is, in fact, my past.

The moment where pure experience happens can exist only without the idea of myself. Can I ever have the time to become aware of what is, without the heavy burden of the past on my shoulders? Without the specious freedom of future ahead of me? It seems the only way to do that is to silence the mind and give no time to myself.

On Enduring Frustration

In my limitations, I am prone to experience frustration.

My physical and mental limits merge into each other, creating a totality called the '*I*'. It is an alluring sensation of intelligence inside my skin, that makes me feel separate from the seemingly unintelligent world around me. My feeling of separation creates an intense need to control my destiny. The roots of the need for control are in my intention to overcome the unpredictability of the environment I am cast to live in. However, I can never fully overcome it, so I get frustrated.

The world around me exceeds my limitations thousandfold with its capacity. I feel threatened by the world because I don't understand it. Resistance arises in me, one thought at a time. When identifying with every thought in my head, an inner conflict blinds me, and I cannot see what the world actually is. Beyond the surface phenomena of thoughts, the world reveals itself to me every moment with all the potential the existence carries within.

My unconsciously arising thoughts create an imaginary world around me. Ignorant of any other kind of a world, I cannot feel myself as I really am behind the veil of thinking. The ravine between the real world and my conceptual world holds the seed of frustration. A beautiful flower called suffering will grow out of that seed.

My frustration and suffering lead me to an unending chase of the next and better moment. The real world around me disappears with my desire to avoid frustration and suffering. As the world vanishes, I build a stronghold around myself, so the mind-made world full of threats cannot see my limitations and vulnerability. As a result, I become fortified against myself.

However, I endure frustration whenever I become aware of who I am without the distraction of thinking. As I am aware of myself, I can see the world around me just as it is. Serene and silent. Nothing more and nothing less.

On Listening to the Inner Echoes

All my experiences are echoes in an empty valley.

Everything fades into silence—the emptiness from whence everything originated in the first place. The brightness of the sun is created when I gaze upon its beautiful shine on the white blanket of snow. As I close my eyes, I can still see the image of the sun in front of me, but it slowly fades away like my breath in the surrounding cold air. Silently it dissolves into the same empty valley of existence it was generated from when I turned my eyes toward it.

The true nature of the present moment always unfolds before my eyes. When I keenly observe my sensory perceptions, I notice how they echo in my mind, and then slowly wane into nothingness. I can still hear the cry of the bird in the silent forest, even though the sound waves are not resonating in my eardrums anymore. I can feel the rough surface of the snow at my fingertips, even though my fingers are not touching the snow anymore. My steps that were just seconds ago crunching on the icy ground are crying for my attention, even though I am already standing still.

My sensory perceptions and experiences turn into echoes instantly after their physical forms are gone. My mind is a record player. It constantly repeats everything that is happening around me, to form an experience suitable for the false identity that bears the name 'I'. When I give my attention to that echo, it feels intense and magical. The mechanics of the form it takes is so sophisticated that my thoughts cannot grasp it. Everything I can do is to be one with that echo.

During the same breath, the echo and I disappear. Sometimes I stay in that state of disappearance. In the emptiness, the echoes of my sensory perceptions do not accumulate in the individual experience of the 'I', but continue their journey into the unknown without me. In my disappearance, I am entirely present. In the silence of the mind, my perceptions of the world arise in the blink of an eye, leaving behind them a wake of things that eventually scatter in the past without sticking to an illusory image of me.

On Loving Myself

I am the most lovable being in this world.

Being alive is an attribute worthy of love. The most important form of love that I can show at any given moment is the love of myself. It is an intimate relationship that connects my thinking and my being. The love of myself is not the kind of love that gives value to my thoughts and deeds depending on how I've succeeded. It is love that looks inward and creates acceptance for my whole existence. Only through that can I find true value in all my thoughts and deeds.

The love for myself is an echo in an empty and endless corridor. It continuously reaches my ears without judgment. It does not hold a grain of egoistic selfishness. As I intensely listen to that echo, I can observe myself being connected to my innermost self. Truthfully speaking, the '*self*' is not even mine. It is not affected by things or time. Whenever I find the deeper self in the empty corridor, I find the unconditional love and compassion for everything surrounding me.

The deeper I journey within myself, the greater part of the surrounding world is included in the idea of myself. However, moments arise when I cannot love myself and be in my own company with full acceptance of myself. During such moments I cannot show pure love for the world around me. If I do not accept myself, the love of all external things is full of requirements and conditions. Any act of love without the pure love of myself is only an effort in fulfilling my personal needs. Trying to reach fulfillment through that kind of needy love is reaching the stars from the sky with my own hand; the hand feels strong, but the stars are utterly out of my reach.

The incessant streams of thinking create moments when I am so blinded by the concept of love, that those personal needs are hidden from my awareness. But during moments of no thoughts, my loving presence is all that remains. It is all that anything in existence needs.

On Approaching the Unknown

My life is a result of my interactions with the unknown.

I have drawn imaginary, yet seemingly realistic borders around the image of myself. It excludes everything that is unknown to me. During every breath I take, I experience new unforeseen happenings that invite me to redefine myself over and over again. That constant redefinition process strengthens the borders of the false identity.

As the sun rises to greet the new day and sheds light on everything the night harbored within, I too can shed light on the world around me. My light, however, turns quickly into a trap that tightens its grip the more I try to get out of it. My mind falls in love with the concepts of freedom, liberation, awakening, and enlightenment. Silently, I start resisting all change. After years of survival battles and a countless number of accumulated self-definitions, my mind has found itself. Now it strives to be unchanging. It seeks to live only in what is known.

The unknown is an inescapable and primordial force. Despite everything the mind creates, the unknown continuously renews beyond the limitations of knowledge. My thinking mind labels everything unknown as a threat to my very existence. As a result, I start feeling uncertainty. I absorb the feeling of uncertainty into myself. It becomes a significant part of my thinking, and whenever I fight against it, I struggle with myself. The 'I' within that is born out of my known thoughts and beliefs lives through my internal conflicts and will do everything it can to prevent a peace treaty within.

My battle is a silent one. It is a distant one. It is like the incessant roar of an ocean far ahead, blown to me by the warm summer's breeze. As I look around, I see myself standing on a battlefield full of lifeless bodies of my false identities. At such moments of clarity, all my uncertainty fades away. I lower my sword and step closer to the unknown. I step closer because I can see my own true nature there.

Without the unknown, I could never feel anything I would experience as myself. Because of that, the unknown is a significant part of me.

On Finding Wisdom in the Unhappiness

My life is full of crests and troughs, and the myriad happenings in between them.

Nothing in the world around me will happen with full certainty. However, that is not my problem. My actual problem is that 'I' do not happen with such certainty as I would like myself to happen. The unpredictable and uncontrollable aspects of myself lead to unhappiness. The occasionally arising lack of happiness is not created in the external world but within myself.

I do not remember unhappiness in the moments of my happiness. Whenever I am happy, the world embraces me with pleasant conditions. Pleasant things rarely create inner resistance. However, the wave-like nature of my life whispers about the certainty of change. Every single crest will give birth to a corresponding trough. When I feel low, when I become aware of the lack of my happiness, an inner resistance arises. I start searching for a scapegoat from the external world.

When my mind grows calm, I can see that my thoughts happen only within me. I can see that they try to defend something that does not need defending. My mind is unconsciously protecting something invulnerable and immortal, into which even time cannot sink its teeth. In reality, my mind is tilting at windmills and engages in a battle that cannot be won.

During my unhappiness, a possibility arises to see the wisdom in the heart of every single moment. My deepest unhappiness carries within the meaning of my brightest exuberance. The depth of the valley of unhappiness defines the height of the mountaintop of happiness. Without my unhappiness, my happiness would not have meaning. My experience at any given moment, even the most dire unhappiness, is only one perspective of my life in the realm of time. And the perspectives are infinitely many.

On Revealing Myself from Behind All the Symbols

That which bears the name 'I' is only a symbol of myself.

My mind lives through symbols—words, numbers, and images. When I think of myself, I think of something I have been in the past, a story of me. These stories carry symbolic meanings I have created myself for myself. They bear as little resemblance to me as my shadow on the ground resembles my body and the sun. The shadow is only a consequence, an interference. The story I keep telling myself about myself has a symbolic nature, just like the shadow which represents the existence of the sun.

Thinking through symbols has caused lots of relatively good things for myself, but it has also led me to a profound state of confusion. Words can never give such a meaning to the world as I hope to find. They cannot give life to me, but blind me from seeing the rich diversity of my life. Words restrict my being, and any restriction will eventually lead to frustration.

I get frustrated fast when I experience myself as a limited being separate from the world around me. As I awaken from the slumber of that frustration—and understand that all existence is seamlessly integrated into one—I gain an entirely different vision in perceiving myself. I see that the 'I' I usually think about is no more me than the image of the sun is the sun. Images can never describe the grandeur of reality. 'I' am a handful of thoughts and beliefs that symbolize something that extends much further and shines much brighter than the image of myself. The mind-made story of the 'I' is only one of my infinite number of faces.

On Moving to the Next Stop

I tend to linger in my present mental position.

I am on a journey to the unknown. A countless number of stops are encountered along the way, each more enchanting and lovable than the last. They whisper into my ears: "Grasp me. I am the truth." I grasp easily because I am uncertain. I make camp in every stop because I fall in love with the knowledge that I am not there alone. Many others have also made their camp in the same stop. The only thing carrying me forward is the natural movement of my feet. One step after another it leads my body and mind toward the unknown.

My transfer to the next stop—to the next mental position—originates from somewhere else than within myself. Something creates interference in my thinking, leading to the birth of the spontaneous movement. It is not forced. It is not decided. Just like the pollen formed in the heart of a flower rises to journey with the wind to unknown lands only to settle in a new place to rest and create life, the spontaneous movement of nature guides my steps.

If I resist the dawn of a new day by plunging deeper into my mind and clinging to a defined image of myself, I unconsciously resist the movement of my feet. The deep and natural desire to renew and move along slips further away from my experience day by day. There are moments when I have almost completely forgotten the movement. The inherent need for life to be one way or the other is all that is. However, such moments of stagnation always precede some greater forces that make my feet move again. Resisting those forces will deepen my anxiety, pain, and suffering.

Life is a series of waves. It holds within moments of consciousness and moments of unconsciousness. Whenever the light of the consciousness brightens, even for an unnoticeable fraction of time, I stop resisting and my mind embarks on its journey toward the next stop. The journey toward the ever-unknown destination continues.

I constantly move toward the understanding that there is nothing else but the beginning, which takes place again and again, moment by moment, never-ending. The understanding is so vast that I cannot *not* attain it. And so, I can move towards mostly in silence.

On Being Aware of Impermanence

I am no longer what I was. I will not be what I am now. I am never what I think I am.

My life is a flame of a candle. When I gaze upon the flame, I adapt to its unpredictable and hypnotic dance. But when I think of the flame, I restrict the natural unfolding of its impermanence. My mind tends to imprison all the spontaneous and continuous happenings into permanent forms.

Whenever a form disappears, the familiar sense of loss arises. The impermanence of all time-bound things is something deeper than a mere thought. It is the essential nature of the eternally renewing present moment. The moment called '*now*' is always changing, yet timeless and unchanging. As I realize it, the conceptual paradox disappears. All my uncertainty and insecurity vanishes, and I accept all the good and the bad happenings just as they are. I accept them as happenings only. I treat them with an open heart and compassion.

Different happenings in my life mean essentially nothing. They gain their meanings only through thinking. Without the interference of my thoughts, I fulfill my role in the vast play of the world without resistance. In my natural state of being, I do not use energy in sustaining good moments or resisting bad moments. Everything is happening in the way it is happening.

Deep under the surface, I am unchanging and permanent. Only from there can I observe the impermanence of the world. Time cannot be without the timeless. Experience cannot be without the experiencer.

On Facing My Problems

I usually find quick and readily available, but deficient,

solutions to the problems I face.

Any solution to a problem that is made without truly facing and accepting the problem is a deficient solution. Such a solution will lead to the reproduction of the problem in the future, only in a different form. As an accumulation of memories, I am limited and unable to face my problems just as they are. In my limitations I usually commit a panic solution, searching for a quick and easy answer. Such an answer can always be found in the past.

Solving a problem while tied to the burdens of the past leads to repeating the same patterns that initially produced the problem. In the heart of every problem I face resides a small and fearful 'I', which is an accumulation of the experiences I have had, or someone else has had. Year after year I find similar solutions to the same, yet seemingly different problems. But deep within the years, a continuous and silent voice echoes in that eternal wheel. It invites me to the other side of all knowledge.

My problems are formed by my small and limited knowledge. When I decide not to resort to my knowledge, an entirely different world opens before me. As I forget everything I know about myself and what I know about the world, I can see my problems as they are in reality.

As I settle in a state of being, where I permit myself to be utterly without knowledge, I discover a level of consciousness that life naturally uses to face itself. Sometimes the solutions that arise from the other side of my knowledge might seem entirely senseless at the moment, but eventually, something much greater will unfold from those decisions. Only by relinquishing my intense need to find immediate and rational answers to my problems, I see my problems as they are.

On Seeing My Myriad Faces

I am an actor in a play which has no beginning or end.

My life constantly flows through different situations in which I choose different roles for myself. Mostly they are roles dictated to me by my personal history. I am a teacher and a student, a father and a son, a master and a slave—whenever my life needs me to be. I am the stillness that fuels everything in existence, and I am a cluster of chaotically appearing thoughts.

The gravity of life pulls me toward itself like the light in the darkness enchants the moth. Whatever situations life bestows upon me, I respond to them with the same inexorable perfection as the situations themselves hold. Occasionally, my ego—the story of me—withdraws timidly closer to myself, and sometimes it is effervescent. At times I am humble, and occasionally I fight. Sometimes I conform, and sometimes I stand rigid like a stronghold.

As I watch with the eyes of inner stillness, it does not matter whether my life is in my hands or if I have admitted it to someone else. In both ways, I fulfill my current life situation in totality, just like it is meant to be. Every force creates a counterforce. Every thought creates a counter-thought. Every breath is the exhalation and inhalation happening in perfect harmony with the flow of the air into and out of my lungs.

My myriad faces in the immeasurably vast play of existence belong to the natural cycle of appearance and disappearance. Whatever role I play—regardless of playing consciously or unconsciously—is the life itself. My role affects life just as much as life affects my role. They are in perfect and utter balance. They are one.

That which affects the world through me has an effect on me. That which has an effect on me affects the world through me.

On Listening to the Voice of My Mind

Thinking is the nature of my mind. Silence is the nature of myself, and it gives life to thinking.

The voice of my thoughts is incessant. It fills my every moment with the stories it tells. Many times, I listen to the words the voice whispers instead of listening to the world around me. The voice of my mind speaks so loudly I cannot hear the world. It blinds me from the natural beauty of the world.

As I gaze upon the still surface of the lake, the voice whispers words of stillness, peace, unknown waters, and all the beautiful reflections my eyes catch. In uneasy situations, it tells me a story of uneasiness, uncertainty, discomfort, and it describes all the dangers created by those feelings. During the moments of loneliness, the voice fills the silence and speaks to me of many situations that have happened, have never happened, or will never happen.

The voice of my mind is always a reflection of my sense of identity. It values, criticizes, judges, and compares the world in relation to myself. The voice constantly assesses what is beneficial or harmful to me, even though in reality it has no ability to recognize true meanings of good or bad. All meanings it whispers into my ears are painfully relative, and never absolute.

Occasionally, moments arise when the voice withdraws. My stream of thought ceases its movement. I awaken from the dream the voice of the mind has created in front of my eyes. The still surface of the lake becomes the stillness itself. The uneasiness of a situation becomes uneasiness itself. The loneliness I feel becomes the solitude itself. They bear no suffocating meanings anymore.

As my mind is rendered silent, I recognize that the world and my thoughts—all the voices that compare the world to myself—happen within me, in my essential being. In silence I have nothing, yet I am everything.

On Believing My Own Feelings

Many of my feelings are products of false experiences.

I am lost in a forest. The light of the day has yielded in front of the deepening night. The trees seem gloomy, uninflected, and even scary as their silhouettes rise in front of the dark and starry sky. I feel something, but my mind cannot refine the right thoughts from the feelings. I repeatedly find myself having experiences that seem just like the trees in that gloomy forest—the profiles are seen, but all the colors are missing.

The pure experience always comes first. It is clear, bright and screaming for attention, but its subtle voice is buried under the thousandfold thoughts of the mind. Excessive thinking turns the pure experience into a blind experience. All I see through the machinery of concepts is the selected memories of what I think I am. Those memories are blind to this moment. Additionally, I transform the blind experience into a false experience, an even more complicated form of experience: "I feel like this, but I should not be feeling like this!" Through the self-denying nature of the false experience, I lose myself in the nocturnal forest.

I start to feel derivative feelings I mistake for real feelings. A life of derivate feelings is full of labels: *me, my, mine, for me, against me, from me to me, by me, of me…* Sometimes those labels are wordless, but they are embedded in every thought I have. They are an expression of my mind-made identity.

There is no need to alter the pure experience and my naturally arising emotions in any way. By abandoning my thoughts, and letting the dead bury their dead, I can step closer to the vivid feeling of liveliness in my heart and meet the reality without the clouds of blind and false experiences. As I am close to the pure experience and see the starry sky above the dark treetops, I can finally commit actions which serve my true self. Through such actions, the whole world gains benefit. The sun can shed its magnificent colors on the land only when the night yields to the light.

I can trust my own feelings only when I realize that nothing real can be defended, nothing real is endangered, and there is nothing unreal in all of existence.

On Ceasing to Resist My Happiness

Happiness is my essential nature.

I am more fond of resisting unknown happiness than letting go of my familiar unhappiness. All the suffering in my life is born out of that resistance. It creates a conflict within that blocks me from finding pure happiness.

My happiness, as I understand it through thinking, is a cloudy sky; if only I could blow the clouds away, I would see the clear and blue sky, and the brightness of the heaven and timeless sun would smile upon me. But the sky is filled with clouds. My happiness is filled with conditions, needs, and requirements. I mistakenly believe that I can find my true happiness only by fulfilling them.

I unconsciously resist my true and unconditional happiness because I cannot let go of the requirements I hold for it. I blindly believe that when the clouds move away, I will finally see the stillness and the peace of the sky. I can never reach lasting happiness through that belief; new clouds always emerge. True happiness is a continuous state of fulfillment, unlike the temporary happiness that emerges only after meeting my requirements for it. In the state of unconditional fulfillment, the sun shines from an open sky every day.

Fulfillment is silent. The happiness it bestows upon me is not found from the top of the most glorious mountain, just as my suffering is not found from the darkest valley of my life. Fulfillment is a paper on which I draw all my mountaintops and dark valleys.

My inner resistance disappears when my need to find happiness disappears. Whenever I can observe the resistance fading, I can see the sun in all its brightness.

On Seeing My Connection to the World

I am eternally alone, but always together.

My death is the cornerstone of all my fears. In my fear I fail to see that death does not mean a departure from this world; death is like falling asleep without never waking up. My birth does not mark my entrance to this world; birth is like waking up without never going to sleep. I am born from the world around me, and I die into the world around me. The 'I', which is the focal point of all my thoughts would not exist if I was never born.

The 'I', who fears death in me and who I think I am, cannot consciously maintain the beat of my heart, breathe while I am asleep, or control my metabolism. I am the sum of countless things significantly greater than I think I am. The air I breathe is the requirement for my continuity. The brightness created by the sun is the foundation of my life. The gravity I feel under my every step is a powerful truth that shapes the physical world I see around me.

The part of me, which abhors death, is a complex structure of blind conditioning. I cannot see my identity because it has raised me to believe what I am. I am not the cause of my identity, but the world around me is. My conditioning is an integrated part of the world. When I identify with the thoughts it whispers into my ears, I plunge deep into the limited and delusional experiences I mistake for life.

As I see my conditioning in bright light—without seeking to change it in any way—I realize my true nature. Silence falls down on my life. Only then can I truly experience my deep connection to the world.

On Understanding the Nature of My Experiences

I lose my experiences by labeling them.

My life is full of waves, like the surface of an ocean. It includes moments of pleasures and sufferings. During the moment of my suffering, I compare the moment with memories of my pleasures. This unconscious thought activity creates an impulse to avoid suffering. Therefore, my pleasures and happiness are seamlessly interconnected with my sufferings and unhappiness.

The effort to erase my suffering has roots in my memories. However, my memory is a deficient tool based on my personal past, and the false sense of identity is limited to what I have seen through the painfully tiny keyhole of my ability to think. Whenever I use my deficient tools in trying to fight my way toward a better moment, my better moment will manifest deficiently in the same way; it will hold within a seed of suffering, which I reactively seek to avoid.

As I become aware of my sufferings just as they are—without labeling them as fear, anxiety, depression, hate, anger, or pain—I break out of the prison of those labels. I cease to be afraid of my fear. I no longer hate my hatred. I stop being depressed because of my depression. The feelings still exist, but I do not derive my identity from them. As I become free of my compulsive thinking, pure experience is revealed. In pure experience, negative feelings become more easily manageable. They could even fade away entirely when my unjudging attention is given to them.

Fire feeds the fire. When I stop fighting my fear with fear, my anger with anger, or my pain with pain, I am no longer imprisoned by a false image of myself. That, which was previously the experience I had tried to get rid of has turned into a fulfilling experience which *is*.

On Noticing My Inner State of Lack

I can never find fulfillment in satisfying my needs.

1 await something in the unknown future to heal my present feeling of lack. The story of myself, narrated by my mind, has created an undefinable state of deficiency. It pulls my needs and desires toward my heart like planets gravitate toward the star. The power of the feeling of lack is continuous, inexorable, and inescapable. If I try to resist it, I end up resisting myself. In resisting myself, I create a deep and unconscious conflict within myself.

My needs will never be satisfied. My search will never come to an end. Truthfully, I do not even know what I am looking for. My mind forces me forward like a strange horse on an unknown road. The only free will that does not imprison me in the endless loop of achieving and becoming is revealed when I take a step back from myself. Only by removing the one that bears the name 'I' from the equation can I observe my unconscious state of lack and the myriad needs that spring from it. My free will manifests in letting my needs exist just as they are, without the smallest effort in changing them.

The 'I' is a tree whose leaves blind me from seeing anything outside. As I take one step further from the tree, I can see all the branches that hold all the leaves. As I take ten steps more, I can see the trunk of the tree from which all the branches grow. As I walk a thousand steps further, the tree becomes just a small silhouette against the horizon, and I can see the world surrounding the tree. And with every step I take, I can feel the ground under my feet, from which every tree grows.

On Accepting My Fragments

The 'I' is a broken mirror; its fragments are glued

together by ignorant beliefs.

That which bears the name 'I' changes with every breath I take. Nothing else exists in my consciousness that would change as fast and as frequently. My sense of identity is a roaring rapid that over millennia carves constant forms in the draw, while never staying the same itself. I experience a change in the world because I am in a continuous flux myself. The change in the world surrounding me is a reflection of the change in my identity.

In the silence of the mind, I become aware that I am not tied to my body, feelings, or thoughts. I break free of their limiting shackles. I notice that the image of the 'I' is only fragments of a mirror spread under my feet. Through those fragments, the 'I' observes the world. My world becomes what I believe those fragments would form if I could repair the mirror back to its unbroken state. But in my incompetence in understanding myself, I cannot do that—not through my mind.

When my compulsive streams of thoughts cease, the need to reassemble the fragments of the 'I' fades away. A pure experience arises. I realize that I am the natural sensation when my bare feet touch the rugged ground. I am the warm experience when I see the face of a smiling baby. I am the complete surrender when I accept the entire world just as it is.

Complete surrender means the death of the false identity from which I have needlessly sought support. I have fought long and unnecessary battles for the 'I'. I have lived in a continuous state of self-defense to protect something that does not need protection. The death of the 'I' is painful and challenging, but as I walk over the fragments of the mirror, a whole new world opens before my eyes. The purpose of that world lays a warm and compassionate blanket over the lifeless form of the 'I'. In every step I take in inner silence, I notice that all the pain and suffering lie under my feet as fragments of my false identity.

On Following My Thoughts

My thoughts create ephemeral images which are not me.

The thoughts flow in front of my eyes like clouds in the light blue sky. As single thoughts, they are quiet, calm, and do not obstruct the beauty my eyes see. They are of no disturbance because I feel they are part of the open sky. However, moments arise when the sky becomes entirely clouded. My thoughts flood into my awareness, creating a veil of thinking I cannot see through. During moments like that, all I have left is a memory of the calmness of the open sky. My mind strives to grasp the experience of the subtle yet boundless joy included in that memory, but never reaches it.

Similarly, as my body consists of innumerable cells supporting each other, my mental positions consist of mutually supportive thoughts. The complex and seemingly highly developed form of life—my state of mind—is an object for the same principles of mechanics that guide the physical world around me. My state of mind stays the same if the world does not apply any external forces toward it. And whenever an external force affects my state of mind, an inner counterforce arises as a reaction. That reaction is an ephemeral image of my false identity.

When my false identity is pushed, it reactively pushes back. When its borders are not honored, it goes into defense mode. The outcome of the situation is only dependent on the force of the thoughts. My false sense of identity follows the same cycle of evolution that all life forms follow—an intricate dance of action and reaction.

This dance of life is essentially a dance of emptiness in which no inner movement exists that could be separate from an outer movement. There is only an all-encompassing movement. The eternal balance of that movement is revealed only in inner silence.

On Touching the Present Moment

The river of my life flows in between the banks of

pleasures and sufferings.

The river banks exist because a river flows between them. The moments of my pleasures are just empty space on the bank of my sufferings, and the moments of my sufferings are gaps on the bank of my pleasures. As my mind shifts between the two banks, it becomes restless. Whenever my mind is restless, I am the restlessness.

Restlessness is a sea of flowers which springs from the seeds of change on the shores. I tend to fall in love with the compelling beauty of such flowers. Embraced by the beauty, I unconsciously become dependent on the inevitable change it bears within. When my mind grasps the pleasures and sufferings on the banks of the river, the experience of time arises. Over time, every experience will evaporate and disappear.

Despite the constant change around me and within me, my essential being in the background is tied to the present moment only. It whispers into my ears that the past and future are just memories and expectations in my mind. If I pay undivided attention to that silent whispering, I can hear it loud and clear.

The whispering tells me that I am not the 'I', which experiences the joy of my pleasures and the dread of my sufferings. I am the seedbed on the river banks where the flowers grow. I stay in the same moment for eternities—the present moment. I am the one who experienced the magnificence of light when my eyes opened for the very first time. I am the one who will take my last breath just before returning back to eternity. I am unchanging. When my mind does not cling and grasp, I can sense the opening, where I am.

On Imagining the World as a Repetition

Every moment is a unique piece of magnificent art.

The continuously unfolding flower of the present moment is unique in the same way as a snowflake is unique. It bears a resemblance to other snowflakes but shares no common details with any of them. The symmetry of a snowflake is as beautiful as the symmetry of birth and death. The interminable cycle of creation, which flows hand in hand with the inevitable destruction of the world is the beginning and the end of all life. No reasons exist within that symmetry for why I should derive my sense of self from the stories connected to my past.

The mind can only offer a simulacrum of my life, where a sense of freshness disappears from everything. I plunge into the illusory images and lead myself astray while believing they are the truth. Similarly, just like how a thousand snowflakes feel identical, or a thousand flowers look alike, or the flames of a thousand candles dance in harmony with the airflow, also my conditioned mind creates an impression of repetition. Every experience of repetition creates limitations, and all limiting beliefs unlock the doors to seemingly endless layers of anxiety, pain, and suffering.

As my mind is rendered silent, I can see how all snowflakes, flowers, and flames are highly unique. I can see the vast diversity of life with my own eyes. I can hear the continuous roar of creation as an ocean, which sends waves straight into the rocky shores of my existence. I can feel the life waving through my entire body in its subtle and undefinable, yet powerful, way. An experience of life beyond the veil of thinking continually forms within me, never ceasing.

A never-ending and never-repeating world arises from behind all the seemingly repetitive and common characteristics of the world of the mind. No such time, place, creature, or life form exists that would be now, or has been in the past, or will be in the future, identical with another or itself. Creation is a ceaseless and ever-continuing cycle of destruction, and I am that.

On Seeing the World in the Colors of a Rainbow

Life happens through myriad empty forms.

My world consists of all the colors I can see when the rays of the sun scatter in the sky above me. Everything I experience through my eyes is a synthesis of those colors, but all the colors are essentially empty. Light does not have a form. However, when it hits my eyes, it gains the form I create for it. A small ray of the sun is formless, yet simultaneously it is the sun itself and all the countless forms where my consciousness breathes.

As I really look at the world around me, I can see beyond those forms. The world is an endless ocean of light which shows me the spectrum of its colors in every single moment when I choose to look directly at it. When I truly gaze at the summer's green lawn or the blanket of winter's white snow on the ground, I can see the unique and ineffable world that surrounds me during my every breath.

As I see the world in its true colors, without clinging to any of the forms created by my mind, I realize how the darkest night gives meaning to the brightest day. Without the experience of a total lack of light, I could never experience the greatest brightness of it. Only by lovingly embracing the darkness can I see where all the light is, and in silence, it scatters in most magnificent colors.

On Seeing Beyond My Life Situation

My life situation happens in time. My life happens now.

I frequently stray in thinking that my life situation is my life. My life situation is many times full of uncertainty and insecurity, created by my memories and the expectations born of my memories. All those things make my mind anxious. Whenever my mind is anxious, the entire world around me becomes an image of anxiety.

If I derive my sense of identity from my life situation, the uncertainty of it arises in me. At times like that, my thoughts reactively breed fear and anxiety. Fear always begets actions, which conflict with my essential nature. Such actions create more fear and anxiety in my life situation.

My continuous striving to achieve the next life situation, that would be somehow better or remained at least the same, makes me forget my life. In my efforts to reach the next moment I become too busy to observe all that is happening now, in the present moment. And the present moment is all that is. Nothing else exists. Fortunately, the deepest essence of my life is untouchable by fear. As I tune into that state of being, I can see the true nature of my fear and suffering, and they no longer hold power to define who I am.

As the stream of compulsive and conditioned thoughts stops, I relinquish the need to identify with my life situation, and I become the life that I am.

On Offering My Help for the World

I am selfish, and all my deeds reflect my selfishness.

I commit virtuous acts because I gain pleasure from them. Also, I mistakenly judge my actions as virtuous because many times I only seek to avoid regret or worry. Committing good deeds only because of personal pleasure, or avoiding guilt, plunges me into a game of power and authority where I create different kinds of dependencies around me.

When I offer my helping hand to another sentient being, I simultaneously create a situation, where another becomes dependent on my help. I unconsciously breed a pattern of authority, which places another being under my authority. My egoistic sense of importance is dependent on the world not deviating from its relationship with my established authority. Deep within, in my unconscious thoughts, I do not want my authority to wane. I feel significant when the world is dependent on me.

As my thoughts fade into silence, my virtuous acts and the help I offer become real. Such help makes the weak stronger and empowers the strong even more. It is true virtue and loving kindness that does not create unnecessary dependencies between the helper and the helped. Instead of offering my helping hand for the fallen, I offer support, enabling a self-caused strengthening. The best cause of my own good deeds is a virtue, which is exercised without the intention of virtue.

On Experiencing Myself as Important

I am not important, I have never been important, and I will never be important.

Different themes are experienced in the great play of my life. They all integrate into the mind-made image of myself. The more dramatic the theme, the more powerfully it affects me. Repetitive great themes become interlocked with me: "I am a loving father, I am a good friend, I am a faithful husband, I am a reliable brother…"

Whenever I make myself important by emphasizing my own role on the stage, I create a fragile construction called the self-image. I become dependent on the world around me. That world is usually insecure, uncertain, and often peaceless. It billows toward me as inexorably as the waves of an ocean hit the shores.

A time will come, eventually, when one of the foundational pillars of my self-image—a repetitive and meaningful theme I have long identified with—will fall. As an inseparable part of myself, the fall will produce collateral damage to other parts of myself also. As one of the meaningful themes in my life turns to sorrow, my whole life easily turns to sorrow. My life is the feelings I feel every day; when I feel suffering, my life is suffering, and when I feel joy, my life is joy.

In the silence of the mind, I can observe that I myself have bestowed the illusion of importance to my role. No one else has given it to me. No one else can ever give it to me. The sense of importance is within me as long as the given theme stays, and the downfall is in me when my life grants me an experience of fierce grace. I am the space where the constant and the inconstant happen simultaneously. I am the space where my life situation arises. I am the stage where the play occurs.

As my mind loses its self-importance, I can see the true nature of the world around me. The world, which is entirely and utterly independent of that which bears the name 'I'.

On Walking Along the Path of

Consciousness

My consciousness breathes freely in the limitless space

where everything happens.

Occasionally, my mind does not feel threatened by the external world. The normal state of mental defense fades away, and the consciousness breaks free from its prison. At first, it expands into my body and observes inner sensations previously dampened by my mind. From my inner body, the consciousness expands to my senses. It observes the world around me without judgment of any kind. Then, the consciousness continues its expansion into the world without limits, and when unlimited, it eventually becomes aware of itself.

When my mind relaxes, that which bears the name '*I*' allows more space for me to breathe. As I breathe in, an ever-greater part of the world is included in the image of myself. Consequently, I feel more compassion toward all things which I previously thought were not included in me. I am not afraid anymore but fall in love with the world, as I fall in love with my self.

Frequently, when something catches my mind's attention, the consciousness plunges back into its imprisonment. I exhale the air out of my lungs, as the unlimited and free perspective of the unjudging consciousness withdraws back into the dream-like fortress of my mind. However, the dream is no longer as deep as it used to be. Consciousness finds it easier to awaken to the world when the veil of sleep has dropped even once. It is no longer imprisoned by the pleasures and sufferings of my mind, but it becomes the space for all the pleasures and sufferings to arise. My mind tries to grasp that state of being, entirely lacking understanding, but eventually, it kneels humbly before the subtle perfection of consciousness.

The purpose of my life is to breathe. When the consciousness has traveled its way into the world free, a primordial and thoughtless realization occurs: the only thing that has always been with me is the consciousness itself. It is my essence, dreaming in the background of my mind and thoughts. It is the space where everything happens. The consciousness is, as I am.

On Living Through Stories

Many times, I live my life carrying a heavy and

redundant burden within.

The 'I' lives through thoughts and stories. It whispers to me that all happenings must have a cause rooted somewhere in the shadows of the past, and so they must affect my unknown future. Those causes and effects in my mind create a set of illusory borders, within which 'I' live, and all the rest happens outside. A sense of separation arises. Any trespassing inside the borders of the 'I' produces conflicts, which inevitably lead to hurt and wounds.

Stories—chaotic syntheses of a countless number of causes and effects—my mind carries within, keep my wounds open. The wounds will never scar if I live my life through the stories. Whenever I identify with my stories, I also force the world around me to live through them, producing similar conflicts that have given birth to those stories in the first place. If I am not aware of their arising, I am repeating my past unconsciously.

When I become aware that the heavy burden of my personal stories presses my posture down, I become free to drop them off my shoulders. As I straighten my back, the air flows better into my lungs. My muscles gain the freedom to relax, supporting only the weight that life can give to itself in its most pristine form. As my body breaks free, my spirit also breaks free because no such dividing line exists between them as I have learned to imagine. When my stories are left behind, my wounds gain a possibility for healing.

Afterward, the scars are still visible, but they are no longer producing pain and suffering. The scars are an integrated part of my body and spirit, which I have accepted in my life. They are warm and silent memories of the stories I once carried with me.

On Falling in Love with My Feelings

My life becomes the expression of my love.

Sometimes the unpredictable life makes me drop to my knees. Fear opens its relentless eyes and turns to anger, grief, anxiety, or dislike toward myself and the present conditions. In the moments, when I hate to be helpless and weak, life will offer me situations where I am helpless and weak. I grow to love my fear so much, that deep within I want it to become my life. Life will always manifest situations that feed the flame of my love.

When I desperately want to be happy, I fall in love with my wanting, which can only exist when I am not happy. When I seek peace, I will never find peace because I have fallen in love with the search for it. When I do all I can to avoid the uncertainty of the unknown future, I will never gain certainty because I have fallen in love with the idea of uncertainty. When I dictate the requirements and conditions for myself to love and be loved, I fall in love with my own requirements. Therefore I can never attain the love I dream about.

Life always shows me the love that I cherish in the depths of my heart. In the moments, when my thoughts stop—when my requirements, conditions, needs, and desires cease to exist—I can experience love as an all-encompassing, infinite openness. It is not a special experience in any way. Love creates foundations for everything special that I have experienced, experience now, or will ever experience.

I sense the foundations of life in myself while loving myself because I am the life. Without me, my experience could never exist at all.

On Giving Up the Need for Control

I am not in control of my life, but I am life itself.

I am the flame of a candle in the wind. I flicker in the direction where the wind is blowing. When the wind is absent, my life is all peaceful. When the wind blows lightly, some small tremors go through my life. I fail to notice them if I do not give undivided attention to myself. When the strong winds blow, my life starts to waver uncontrollably in directions I never could have imagined. A possibility also exists that a storm arises, sweeping the whole flame into nothingness.

I am prone to experience frustration when the wind blows in a direction where I do not want or expect it to blow. Sometimes I feel powerless and unable to control the capricious paths of life. At other times, all life seems to be under the spell of my ability to control it, and nothing happens in conflict with what I have decided. Both experiences—the control and the lack of control—are the same. They are but different perspectives of one experience.

That, which bears the name 'I', has cut off the umbilical cord of life. It expects to control life but experiences profound suffering when the expectations are not met. It cannot accept that life includes a countless number of forces that are unattainable and uncontrollable by it. The 'I' does not remember that even amid the most furious storm, the light of consciousness that has created the 'I' shines brightly in the surrounding chaos. This light never disappears.

The flame of the candle does not expect the wind to blow from any special direction. As the wind blows, the flame does not ask why it blows. The flame does not question where the wind is coming from, where it is going to, or what will be the next direction it blows in. The flame accepts the wind entirely just as it is, and bends without resistance to the direction where it is supposed to bend. While bending, the flame shows its true nature and power.

On Listening with the Ears of My Needs

My needs restrict and limit the world of my experiences.

My needs and hopes define what sounds reach my ears. Often, I hear only what satisfies my needs, soothes my suffering, and gives me pleasure. Through it all, I can hear only my own voice; the incessant voice inside my head, which continuously strives for lasting happiness. However, it can never reach happiness with the tools it has.

My subtle feelings of dissatisfaction toward the present moment color everything the world humbly and sincerely gives to me. My conditioning and beliefs are filters, letting only such things through the gates of my mind that serve my conditioning and beliefs. While listening through them, I can hear only countless echoes from the past which act as the foundation for my current conditioning and beliefs. I plunge into a vicious loop of the human mind.

As my mind grows silent and its striving to avoid suffering disappears, I can hear everything. I hear the swish of the leaves in the light wind, the distant singing of the birds in the spring morning, the voices of my loved ones when they direct their words toward me, the dog barking somewhere far away, the random passerby's steps in the tarmac street, the cry of a small baby, my breathing, the beating of my heart, the subtle ringing of my ears, and the distant background noise that life creates in all its diversity. I can hear the liveliness of life in all the capacity my ears have given me.

Listening is essential only after my own needs and desires have faded away. Only then can I hear the world as it desires to be heard, and as it truly is—in the way that I truly am.

On Choosing My Own Thoughts

Thoughts gravitate toward me, and they bear

resemblance to the thoughts I already harbor within.

My thoughts always attract more thoughts, which play the same melody. Loving thoughts attract more loving thoughts. Fearful thoughts attract more fearful thoughts. Selfless thoughts attract more selfless thoughts. Selfish thoughts attract more selfish thoughts. Creative thoughts attract more creative thoughts. Destructive thoughts attract more destructive thoughts.

My thoughts grow as any living being grows—they accumulate over time. When enough thoughts are clustered together, they form myriad mental positions, opinions, and truths. The forms of my thoughts affect my emotions, which reflect in the world around me. Eventually, all the reflections loop back as the forms of my thoughts. Loving thoughts create more love around me, and fearful thoughts generate more fear around me. The world always responds to my mental positions by creating the conditions which reflect my emotions and thoughts. It happens without valuing, judging, criticizing, or comparing, and before all, it happens with full certainty.

I cannot consciously choose the conditions the world bestows upon me, but from the silence and stillness of my mind, I can choose my own thoughts. In choosing my thoughts, I can affect the reality my world is offering me. And what magnificent and unrivaled freedom it is to choose my own thoughts instead of allowing thoughts happen to me.

The world is a vehicle helping me to express the thoughts I am carrying within. It is a mirror in which I look deep into my own eyes.

On Seeing the True Nature of My Virtues

True virtue is not found in repeating virtuous acts.

What I usually consider as my virtues are mechanical processes, which have very little connection to true virtues. My mind is full of patterns with an investment of the '*I*' within. Therefore, the virtues it has created are based on valuing, comparing, and judging. A virtue that has foundations in the value-based personal world of mine is not true virtue. Such virtue is not sincerely and whole-heartedly beneficial to the world around me.

True virtue emerges from thoughtlessness. True virtue does not rely on the concept of time. Its nature transcends causes and effects and steadies itself in the focal point of all life, the moment called '*now*'. As the mind is silent and inner stillness prevails, my actions hold a seed of true virtue. My actions are not truly virtuous unless their consequences are unlimitedly beneficial. When I exercise truly virtuous acts, I do not follow the requirements, rules, and conditions dictated by the world around me.

Only when I break out of the imprisonment of my own blind beliefs, can I see all the things clearly which I have considered as my virtues. They do not necessarily disappear, but they gain new forms and produce new kind of actions—actions, which the one that bears the name '*I*' is incapable of. Pristine virtue is not limited by my thinking. It is independent of all my thoughts, especially the thoughts concerning the 'I'. True virtue arises spontaneously in me, is unleashed in the world through me, and holds no expectations of its consequences ever returning back to me.

True virtues are not mechanical. They have neither past nor future. They occur in the present moment spontaneously as an action, not a reaction. They create fertile ground for more focused, loving, and unjudging thoughts to blossom.

On Setting Aside My Knowledge

The deeper I listen, the clearer I can hear the silence.

As I listen to the myriad sounds in the world around me, many times I listen to the voice of my own thinking. In the pure experience, the bird is not "a bird", the snowflake is not "a snowflake", the tree is not "a tree", the sky is not "the sky", beautiful is not "beautiful", hideous is not "hideous". The words are only concepts my mind has created for things arising and falling inside my consciousness. Those concepts veil me inside their opaque noise, obstructing me from seeing, hearing, and feeling the world as it really is.

My life is a rich experience—significantly richer than my thoughts can ever describe—and it is buried below all the things I have accumulated in the paths of my life. The world lingers silently below the blanket of my own knowledge. My knowledge has accumulated within me through learning, and most of what I have learned has been forced into me. The knowledge driven into me with force—my conditioning—accumulates over time and becomes an intrinsic part of my self-image. When I watch the world through my self-image, I try to force the world around me to adopt the form of my knowledge.

If I really desire to hear, see, or feel, I have to set aside my knowledge—*all of it.* I am incapable of doing so with my willpower because it just depletes my energy and empowers the '*I*' that is sustained by my knowledge. I can only set aside my knowledge by becoming aware that my knowledge exists. As I become aware of the '*I*', that has taken the form of my knowledge, I consequently become aware of my self. The self is seen only through what is not the self.

I feel the primordial silence flow within me when my accumulated knowledge recedes. The world in front of my eyes adopts a form of ultimate and actual reality. It kneels in front of me in the ever-present space and time, which is called '*here and now*'.

On Letting My Mind Grasp Thoughtlessness

My mind holds a compulsive interest for silence within.

Whenever I see my life without the veil of blinding thoughts, my mind becomes interested in it. My thoughtlessness happens in a space my mind does not have authority over. It quickly forms a concept describing the spaciousness within, which it then defines desirable and beneficial for me.

After my mind has formed a concept about the thoughtless space within me, it strives to attain that space for itself. It guides me toward a thoughtless state of mind. I usually do not notice how that guidance is a thought in itself, with which I identify easily because of all the promises it holds within. I imprison myself in that thought, which can at best point to the thoughtless spaciousness in me. I come to a standstill in the crossroads of the mind and silence, staring at a signpost to an unknown destination that is not marked on my map. Silence is a destination I can never understand or reach through my cherished ability of thinking. I make the signpost into a symbol for a peaceful state of being where no thoughts and intellectual pride takes place. I start adoring and worshipping the signpost, never reaching the true silence within.

However, my mind does not lead me to such illusions intentionally. It does not shackle me because it is evil or wanting to cause me suffering. It only represents the accumulated knowledge, which has given birth to the 'I' within in the first place. The 'I' is a symbol for myself, filled with noise of relative knowledge. All relative knowledge I bear within is prone to create an illusory experience of a separate me.

As I live in harmony with my mind, I can live in harmony with the world around me. Within that harmony, my mind no longer uses me, but I use my mind whenever I need it. I think only when I decide to think. Only through that can true change and transcendence take place.

On Trusting in My Search

The search for myself is one of the most spectacular delusions my mind has created.

A desire to believe in something greater than myself screams within me. I believe I can attain a greater state of existence by exercising the right things in the right way. I am constantly looking for something to make me accept myself more permanently. I continuously wait for the better moment that would be the climax of my whole life, that would repair my defective past as it seems now. A concept of enlightenment or spiritual awakening is something my mind plays with, weaving beliefs and mental positions around it, only to protect the hidden mechanisms of my mind.

Occasionally, I believe I have no ego. When that belief arises and becomes a thought within me, I have already been deceived by my mind. The basic defense mechanism of my mind is to raise itself to be a servant of a seemingly higher level of consciousness, whenever its nature is about to be revealed. It does not want to be revealed because the revelation would mean the end of the 'I'. Just like any living being, so too wants the mind-made 'I' to stay alive. Therefore, the dream of thinking remains painfully strong.

Clinging to an idea of a seemingly higher level of being is not good or bad. This idea is only included in me. It winds within me like the path, which I journey through the forests of my life. It is profoundly connected to a concept called time, which I experience from different perspectives of the past and future.

As I turn my focus to the focal point of all my experiences—my *self*—time ceases to be. Without time, I do not even have to get rid of my ego or thoughts. They are parts of me and included in me similarly as the perspective of time is included in me. In totally accepting my ego, its authority over me evaporates. My mind calms down. I find out that the mind longs for compassionate attention, which it cannot give to itself.

In the silence of my mind, I become aware that nothing greater than me exists; nothing exists outside of me. Therefore, my essential nature cannot be defined.

On Being

Being continually unfolds in the present moment.

I am not what I believe I am. My identification with beliefs conditions me to serve an imaginary world of the past that was created by other people.

I am not what I think I am. My identification with thoughts casts me into their symbolic and limited world.

I am not my opinions. My identification with opinions imprisons me to protect my thoughts and beliefs.

I am not what others think I am. My identification with other people's words restricts me into their thoughts and opinions.

I am not my feelings. My identification with feelings turns me into a frustrated being, limited by conditions.

I am not my body. My identification with the body limits me as a creature separate from the surrounding world.

I am not my memories and expectations. My identification with memories and expectations cast me into the river of time, confining me to mind-made illusions of time.

I am not me. My identification with the false image of myself, the mind-made 'I', leads me to illusory waves of pleasures and sufferings where I settle for a delusional image of my own life.

As all the definitions of myself disappear,

the stillness arises from beyond the mind.

My loving presence is all that remains.

In the soothing silence, I am.

www.ingramcontent.com/pod-product-compliance
Lightning Source LLC
LaVergne TN
LVHW091557170726
843492LV00007B/2163